This journal belongs to:

_____

the
minimalist-*ish*
journal

the
minimalist-*ish*
journal

Buy Less, Live Better, and Find Joy
in What You Already Have

Christina Mychas

A TarcherPerigee Book

tarcherperigee

an imprint of Penguin Random House LLC
1745 Broadway, New York, NY 10019
penguinrandomhouse.com

Most TarcherPerigee books are available at special quantity discounts for bulk purchase for sales promotions, premiums, fundraising, and educational needs. Special books or book excerpts also can be created to fit specific needs. For details, write SpecialMarkets@penguinrandomhouse.com.

Art and design by Katie Kavanagh

Trade paperback ISBN: 9780593717134
Ebook ISBN: 9780593855126

Printed in the United States of America
1st Printing

The authorized representative in the EU for product safety and compliance is Penguin Random House Ireland, Morrison Chambers, 32 Nassau Street, Dublin D02 YH68, Ireland, https://eu-contact.penguin.ie.

contents

introduction

Hi, I'm Christina, and I'm a shopaholic. No, not in that cutesy "shopping is my cardio" kind of way. For as long as I could remember, I felt I needed to go shopping. I shopped when I was happy, sad, bored—you name it. But with my closet overflowing and my bank account always in the red, I started to notice more stuff always became more stress, more overwhelm, and a lot more debt. Instead of being excited about the purchases that were supposed to make me happy, I found myself in a constant cycle of stressing about money, going shopping to relieve that stress, and then doing it all over again. I had no control over my impulses, my emotions, or my money. Something needed to change.

That was when I discovered "No Buy," a no-spend challenge that we'll dive into later in this journal. No Buy eventually brought me to minimalism, which for a long time I saw as the perfect solution to my shopping problem. After all, if I never found what I was looking for in more, then surely I'd find my answer in less! And for a while, minimalism worked great! I got rid of 60 percent of my clothes, I stopped shopping completely, and I even paid off my final $80,000 of debt in two and a half years! Like, wow! But just like I took my shopping habits too far, I noticed the same thing happening with minimalism. Like a yo-yo dieter, I once again found myself missing balance.

That's when I landed on the Minimalist-ish Method, which uses minimalism as a tool to help you find more with less—not with nothing. I made all the mistakes on both ends of the extreme so you don't have to. In this journal we'll explore your relationship with your shopping and your stuff. We will work on shifting your habits from impulsive to intentional, and we'll focus more on what you already have. So I hope you'll use this journal to plan and reflect on your journey toward simplifying with more balance. Always remember, you are enough as you are. We're just getting rid of everything that's in the way.

Christina Mychas | CEO
Minimalist-ish

PART 1:
the minimalist-ish method

"

*The ability to simplify means to
eliminate the unnecessary so that
the necessary may speak.*

—Hans Hofmann

Welcome to *The Minimalist-ish Journal*! If you picked up this book, it's probably because you're sick of overspending, clutter, or compulsive shopping on one hand, but on the other hand, you don't want to go so minimalist that you feel bored or deprived. Well, you've come to the right place. This journal will help you . . .

Stop focusing on the stuff

This journal is designed to help you shift your mindset from one of scarcity to one of abundance. Through mindful reflection, *The Minimalist-ish Journal* will help you develop a new appreciation for what you *already have* so you can shift your focus away from *what's next*.

Build intentionality

Say goodbye to buyer's remorse! With the structure to help you plan, track, and implement your goals, *The Minimalist-ish Journal* makes planning for your next buy as easy as filling in the blanks. You'll find that when you have the right framework, being deliberate about your spending will become second nature.

Realize your goals

With my balanced approach, *The Minimalist-ish Journal* will help you discover how to simplify your lifestyle in a way that works for *you*. This includes realistic and actionable steps to turn your goals into a reality, without having to change who you are in the process.

The journal, which will help you make, achieve, and celebrate Minimalist-ish goals on a weekly, monthly, and quarterly basis, begins on page 39. But don't flip there just yet! First, you'll want to understand the Minimalist-ish Method that makes this journal so effective.

I call it "Minimalist-*ish*" because many of us tend to have a certain idea of what minimalism is *supposed* to look like and then feel bad when we fail to achieve that vision. It's usually some highly curated version of reality that's much easier to *imagine* than to actually *live*. So I decided, "What would it be like if we went *-ish?*"

Minimalist-ish is a little bit of minimalism, a whole lot of intentionality, and none of the *miserable*-ism. With the Minimalist-ish Method, you can embrace the traditional minimalist value of finding more with less, without feeling the pressure to turn that less into *nothing*. It means you can have as big a wardrobe as you want (**in any color you want!**). It means you can buy something new just because you want to (even if it doesn't serve a practical need). It means you can let go of what no longer serves you but *happily* keep the rest. When you start to give yourself *permission* to keep the things you love because you love them for you, that's when simplifying can really start to get . . . simple.

The Minimalist-ish Method is an easy five-step system that I encourage you to keep top of mind as you work through this journal. It can be broken down like this:

01 *Set the intention for your dream life*

What does your ideal life look like? How do you want to feel every day? What does your schedule look like? What outfits are you wearing? What is your bank account balance? When you create the vision of your dream life and keep it in mind, the action you'll need to take to make it reality will follow.

02 *Figure out what you have*

Before you let go of what's in the way, you need to get an idea of what you have right now. Focus on what you want to *keep*, not what you think you should let go of. The Minimalist-ish Method is not about *how much* stuff you have; it's about making space for all the beautiful things you want to *keep*.

03 *Declutter the excess*

You don't have to get rid of anything you don't want to, but I believe it's a good idea to get rid of anything that no longer brings you joy or value. These items served their purpose at one time, and it's okay if they no longer do. Sell, repurpose, or donate these items. Put anything you're not sure about into storage. This way you're still addressing any visual clutter, and you can always revisit these items later.

04 *Fall in love with the now*

In this journal, we'll be focusing a lot on how to mindfully bring new things into your life without guilt, but that's not a reason to forget about what you already have. After all, you brought all the things you currently own into your life for a reason. We'll be setting goals, creating wish lists, and more in this journal, but remember, it's not always about what you can vs. what you cannot buy. Because when you're always focused on what's next, it will be really hard to be happy with what you have right now.

05 *Be picky*

The Minimalist-ish Method isn't about saying no to yourself all the time. There's definitely a time and a place to make sacrifices to meet your goals, but there's also a time to acknowledge all your hard work and to have some fun. I believe being intentional about what you buy also means you don't settle. Wait, create a plan, and make that purchase one you won't regret. I don't do buyer's remorse over here!

FINDING YOUR WHY

Before you start writing reflections, setting goals, and decluttering your closet, let's take a step back. Ask yourself: "But, *why*?" Let's keep it real here. If you don't have a good why, you won't be motivated enough to make the changes you want. Heck, you may not even be motivated enough to use this journal! When I was a full-blown shopaholic, I was also in over $120,000 of student loan debt. Yikes, right? I was constantly worried about money, but I never made any progress because of my compulsive shopping habit. So the why that started it all for me was to finally get control of my spending and become debt free. Your why is everything. It's going to be your reason to start *and* your reason to keep going to reach your goals.

Use the following spread to write down your big why. And then ask "Why?" to that why. The more specific the why, the better. The deeper you dig, the clearer your goal becomes. Knowing this with clarity will make it easier to help you build those habits and simplify, because now you know *why* you're changing your behavior and doing the hard things to reach your goal.

Common whys

Some of the most common whys people have for going Minimalist-ish include:

- to become a more conscious consumer

- to build more environmentally sustainable habits

- to save more money or pay down debt

- to cultivate appreciation/gratitude for what they already own

- to learn to shop their closet more

- to learn to slow down and recognize their impulses or triggers

- to discover new, more meaningful ways to spend their time

EXAMPLE WHY

How do you find your why? Let's look at the example of paying off debt.

What's my goal?

To pay off my debt

Why?

Because I'm constantly stressing about money, and it never feels like I have enough.

What would I do with my money if I wasn't in debt? (Get specific here and dream big. No judgment! This is where you're manifesting your big goals just for you!)

I would go on my dream vacation to Italy for one month. I would fly direct, take a pasta-making class, and try a new flavor of gelato every night.

How much debt do I have?

$10,000

So what's my big why?

To pay off $10,000 of debt so I can worry less about money and plan my dream vacation to Italy

TRY IT YOURSELF

What's my goal?

_____

_____

_____

Why?

_____

_____

_____

How will my life be different when I reach my goal?

_____

_____

_____

What will I do with my time instead?

_____

_____

_____

So what's my big why?

_____

_____

_____

Use this space to write out, draw, plan, and find your why.

FINDING YOUR HOW

Now that you know your why, it's time to think about your how. Your why helps you set your goal; your how helps you achieve it. Here's a five-step process to help you find your how.

STEP 1:

Write out your goal from the last section—be as specific as possible!

I want to pay off $5,000 of credit card debt.

STEP 2:

Write down your big why from the last section.

Because I'm tired of feeling crushed by debt, and I want to actually be able to save money to travel once a year.

STEP 3:

Write down your when—again, the more specific, the better.

I want to pay off $5,000 of credit card debt over the next ten months.

STEP 4:

Write down your how. Your how is the system you will rely on every day to make progress toward your goal. If your goal is your target, your system is the way to hit it. What do you need to do (or stop doing) every day to achieve it in your set timeframe?

I need to find or free up an extra $500 a month in my budget over the next ten months to meet my goal.

Things I can do to get an extra $500 per month:

- Stop using the credit card I'm trying to pay off and switch to cash and debit.

- Declutter and sell things I no longer need to make extra money.

- Cut takeout costs by meal planning and bringing my own lunch to work.

- Write a budget every month to make sure my money goes where I need it to go to reach my goal.

STEP 5:

Put it all together! Declare your goal to yourself by writing it down here in an "I will" statement. Combine your goal with your system and start taking action to make it happen!

I WILL pay off $5,000 of credit card debt in the next ten months. I will do this by budgeting at the beginning of every month, and putting an extra $500 down on my credit card. To get the extra $500 I need each month, I WILL:

- Plan meals and lunches during the week.

- Limit takeout and restaurants to twice a month.

- Stop putting MORE money on this credit card and use cash/debit instead.

- Temporarily stop shopping for new clothes and shop my closet instead.

- Declutter once every two to three months and sell what's in good shape.

- Put more time into my side hustle to generate extra income to pay off my debt.

And that's how you couple goal setting and system building to achieve your vision. The clearer you are on your goal, the easier it will be to map out your system to achieve it. Use the following pages to map out some of yours!

TRY IT YOURSELF

My goal is . . .

_____

_____

_____

My big why . . .

_____

_____

_____

What is my timeline?

_____

_____

_____

What will I do with my time instead?

_____

_____

_____

What is my how?

_____

_____

_____

What is my "I will" statement?

Use this space to write out, draw, plan, and find your how.

LOW BUY VS. *NO* BUY

Now that you know your why and your how, it's time to set some simple rules around your buying habits. Depending on your personal goals and tendencies, you can either do a No Buy challenge or a Low Buy challenge. What's the difference?

NO BUY IS . . .

a strict commitment to eliminating excessive spending from your budget. It means you won't buy any items in categories you don't truly need more of, like clothing, makeup, or skincare.

If you have a tendency to follow rules and find the most success when you go all in to a challenge, No Buy may be for you.

LOW BUY IS . . .

a less restrictive take on a No Buy. You're allowed to buy things in your favorite categories; you just set a predetermined limit on how much or how often.

If a No Buy seems too daunting, too restrictive, or too "cold turkey," then a Low Buy may be a better choice!

LOW BUY/NO BUY RULES

Examples of No Buy or Low Buy Categories
(Choose one, two, or all, if you're feeling ambitious!)

- clothing

- makeup

- skincare

- haircare

- takeout

- home decor

- jewelry and accessories (bags, hats, belts, etc.)

- hobby supplies

- video games

- subscription boxes

Now let's set some rules around your chosen categories.

Examples of No Buy Rules

- Pay with cash or debit only.

- Buy only replacement items. You have to use up that eyeshadow palette before buying a new one.

- Gift cards are okay to buy replacement items with.

- It's okay to buy gifts for others.

Examples of Low Buy Rules

- You're allowed to buy two items of clothing per month, but you must sell or donate one old item first.

- You must pay cash or be able to pay off your purchase on your credit card in full if you buy.

- You must wait one week before buying.

- You can buy secondhand items only.

- You must cook three dinners at home to be able to buy one takeout dinner on the weekend.

- You must be able to create at least three wearable makeup looks if you buy the palette.

- Pants and skirts *must* have pockets or you won't buy them.

Remember, this challenge is *not* about deprivation or about punishment for your past overconsumption. It's an exercise to gain insights on your current consumption and spending habits. It's also an exercise in gratitude, making a conscious effort to use what you have to its fullest. Be sure to find the *abundance* as you work through your planner. I am *not* about the mindset of "I should," of "OMG what a waste," or of guilt here. Even if you slip up on day one, it doesn't mean it's over. One day, one hour, one minute at a time.

LOW BUY/NO BUY: QUESTIONS TO ASK YOURSELF BEFORE YOU BUY

Intentional spending is all about pausing to make sure you're thinking about a purchase before you make it. Use this spread to write out your Low Buy Questions cheat sheet. Refer back to these questions whenever something catches your eye.

Examples of pre-purchase questions

- Do I *really* want or need this? (Is it a *"Hell yes!"*?)

- What exactly is it about this thing that intrigues me? Why?

- How will my life be different once I buy this thing?

- Will I wear or use this a year from now?

- Am I happy to spend this money guilt-free?

- Can I wait *at least* twenty-four hours before I buy?

- Is this the best use of my money right now?

- Who am I buying this for? (Me? My fantasy self? Someone else?)

HOT TIP

Before buying new clothes, ask yourself, "Will I wear this at least thirty times?" If the answer is an honest yes, then make your plan to buy it!

Use this space to write out your own Low Buy/No Buy Questions.

DATE:

MY LOW BUY/NO BUY RULES

Write down some of your own rules—remember, what you say goes!

I WANT TO DO:
(Circle one)

LOW BUY | NO BUY

TIMELINE

My general timeline for waiting to buy something is . . .

(Circle one or specify below)

1 DAY | 1 WEEK | 1 MONTH

_____

WHY?
(Select reasons that resonate or write your own)

☐ To change my spending habits

☐ To change my relationship to consumption

☐ To live a more sustainable, environmentally friendly life

☐ To cultivate gratitude for what I already have

_____

_____

CATEGORIES
(Select categories or write your own to apply your rules to)

☐ Clothing   ☐ Makeup   ☐ Haircare   ☐ Skincare

☐ Jewelry   ☐ Accessories ☐ Home Decor   ☐ Takeout

_____ _____ _____ _____

_____ _____ _____ _____

_____ _____ _____ _____

_____ _____ _____ _____

RULES
(Select your rules or write your own)

☐ I am allowed to buy _____ (quantity) per _____ (day/week/month/year)

☐ I am allowed to spend _____ ($) per _____ (day/week/month/year)

☐ I should have _____ ($) in my savings (or paid off on debt) before I buy
_____ (item)

☐ If an item costs more than _____ ($), then I will wait _____ (time)
before buying it

☐ If I feel like I've failed, I will remind myself that . . .

_____

_____

_____ *(affirmation)*

☐ Other rules (specify)

_____

_____

EXCEPTIONS
I can exercise leniency when it comes to the following . . .

☐ I've completely run out of an item   ☐ An item broke

☐ I've decluttered one old thing   ☐ I can use points or a gift card
(the one-in, one-out decluttering rule)   to buy an item

_____   _____

_____   _____

_____   _____

_____   _____

DATE:

MY LOW BUY/NO BUY RULES

Write down some of your own rules—remember, what you say goes!

I WANT TO DO:
(Circle one)

LOW BUY | NO BUY

TIMELINE

My general timeline for waiting to buy something is . . .

(Circle one or specify below)

1 DAY | 1 WEEK | 1 MONTH

_____

WHY?

_____   _____
_____   _____
_____   _____
_____   _____
_____   _____
_____   _____
_____   _____

CATEGORIES

_____ _____   _____ _____
_____ _____   _____ _____
_____ _____   _____ _____
_____ _____   _____ _____
_____ _____   _____ _____

RULES

_____
_____
_____
_____
_____
_____
_____
_____
_____
_____
_____
_____
_____
_____
_____
_____
_____
_____

EXCEPTIONS

_____   _____
_____   _____
_____   _____
_____   _____
_____   _____
_____   _____
_____   _____
_____   _____

PLANNING FOR IMPERFECTION

So you impulse bought—now what? First of all, it happens! Forgive yourself! What you're doing is not easy. The path toward sustainable change takes time, patience, and a whole lot of mistakes along the way. Either way, it's good to have a plan in place for times like these. Use these emergency pages if you're ever feeling tempted to overspend or if you just feel like you're falling off the wagon. I've laid out some things to consider below, but feel free to write out your own contingency plan for when the going gets tough.

SO YOU IMPULSE BOUGHT. WHAT DO YOU DO?

Go back to your Low Buy/No Buy Questions—have you been asking yourself these questions before you buy? Why or why not? What do you need to do differently? Be honest with yourself.

_____

_____

_____

_____

_____

_____

_____

_____

_____

_____

_____

_____

_____

Revisit your Low Buy/No Buy Rules—are your rules realistic? Or do you need to make some changes? Set yourself up for success—keep it challenging but doable!

_____

_____

_____

_____

_____

_____

_____

_____

_____

Lay out the facts. Did you actually fail? Is feeling guilty helping? How can you turn this around with compassion for yourself?

_____

_____

_____

_____

_____

_____

_____

_____

_____

_____

_____

Where in the shopping process do you feel like you're stumbling: online browsing, stress shopping, social media scrolling? What can you change here?

_____

_____

_____

_____

_____

_____

_____

_____

What's your why? What's holding you back from it?

_____

_____

_____

_____

_____

_____

_____

_____

_____

_____

_____

_____

SHOULD I BUY THIS? CHEAT SHEET

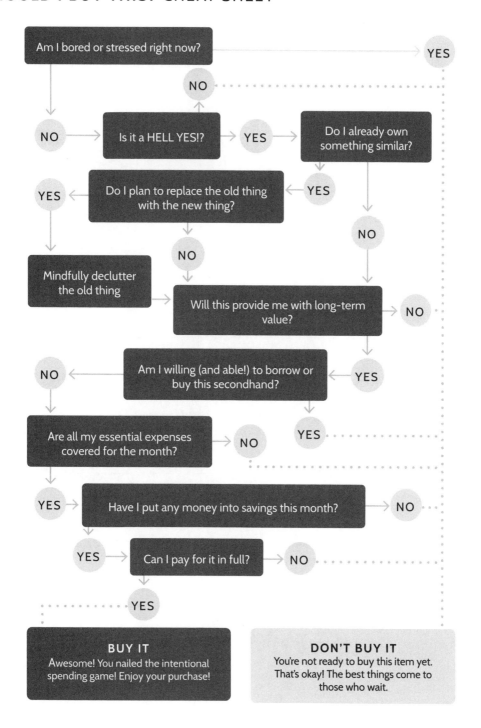

Am I bored or stressed right now? — YES

NO

Is it a HELL YES!? — YES → Do I already own something similar?

NO

Do I plan to replace the old thing with the new thing? ← YES

YES

NO (Do I already own something similar?)

Mindfully declutter the old thing

NO (replace the old thing)

Will this provide me with long-term value? — NO

YES

Am I willing (and able!) to borrow or buy this secondhand? ← YES

NO

YES

Are all my essential expenses covered for the month? → NO

YES

Have I put any money into savings this month? → NO

YES

Can I pay for it in full? → NO

YES

BUY IT
Awesome! You nailed the intentional spending game! Enjoy your purchase!

DON'T BUY IT
You're not ready to buy this item yet. That's okay! The best things come to those who wait.

THINK AHEAD

Consider these questions and scenarios that might come up during your Low Buy or No Buy challenge.

How will I get the most out of what I already own?
(e.g., Do one new makeup look each week with my own stash, shop my closet once a week for a new outfit and take a selfie)

_____

_____

_____

_____

_____

_____

_____

What is my "slipup" plan? What will I do if I give in and buy something on my No Buy list? What will I say to myself? How will I reset?

_____

_____

_____

_____

_____

_____

_____

_____

_____

_____

Use this space to write out, draw, and plan for a slipup.

ABUNDANCE MINDSET

So you've committed to a Low Buy or No Buy challenge, and now you're super excited to go all in. But let's take a step back for a second to make sure you're approaching this challenge from a mindset of abundance rather than one of scarcity. This is where most people go wrong with this challenge, so here's what *not* to do with your intentional-spending challenge this year:

- Don't view it as a punishment for previous "bad" spending.

- Avoid "panic buying"—as in, getting in your last shopping spree before starting your challenge. Ease yourself into it.

- Don't make it all about the stuff—you will have a hard time with this challenge if all you're focused on is what you're allowed vs. not allowed to buy.

Instead of viewing your intentional spending challenge from a perspective of "I can have this" vs. "I can't have this," shift your mindset into one of abundance. Low Buy and No Buy is *not* about the stuff. Heck, it's not even really about shopping. It's about finding joy and satisfaction in the many things you already have. Use the following pages to make a plan for your abundance mindset in your No Buy or Low Buy. This is to help you reframe old judgments you may have about yourself and your habits. How can you change a negative judgment into a positive action plan?

HOW DO I **CURRENTLY** FEEL ABOUT:

My possessions:

_____

_____

_____

_____

_____

_____

_____

_____

_____

_____

My spending habits:

_____

_____

_____

_____

_____

_____

_____

_____

_____

_____

_____

HOW I **WANT** TO FEEL ABOUT MY POSSESSIONS AND SPENDING HABITS:

What do I need to change about my possessions to feel better about them?
(e.g., Do one new makeup look each week with my own stash, shop my closet
once a week for a new outfit and take a selfie)

_____

_____

_____

_____

_____

_____

_____

What do I need to change about my spending to feel better about it? Is there
anything I can spend less on so I can spend more on what I really value?

_____

_____

_____

_____

_____

_____

_____

_____

_____

_____

_____

LOOKING AT MY CURRENT COLLECTION:

What do I love about it? Why?

_____

_____

_____

_____

_____

_____

_____

_____

What do I want to change about it? How?

_____

_____

_____

_____

_____

_____

_____

_____

_____

_____

_____

PART 2:
the minimalist-ish journal

"

We buy things we don't need with money we don't have to impress people we don't like.

—Dave Ramsey

HOW TO USE THIS JOURNAL

Monthly Overview

Now that you understand the Minimalist-ish Method, you're ready to start journaling! But first, here's a rundown of how this journal is set up and how to use its features to achieve your Minimalist-ish goal.

PREPARING FOR THE MONTH AHEAD

I love a good bird's-eye view of the month ahead. Each calendar in this journal is completely customizable. Fill in the dates on the calendar, and personalize it to your month. Helpful dates to consider are:

- Paydays

- Birthdays and social events

- Important bills—write down due dates!

- Appointments: medical, beauty, hair, self-care

- Travel

- Don't forget unusual expenses! Any annual fees coming up this month? Oil changes? Snow tires?

- No Buy or Low Buy days (*That's right! You can set your own Low Buy timeline. If you're on the fence, try challenging yourself to one No Buy day a month and increase from there!*)

Every month, I've also included a theme with an optional challenge you can try to help you along your Minimalist-ish journey. Feel free to customize and plan out your challenges as you like!

You can find *optional* monthly challenges here

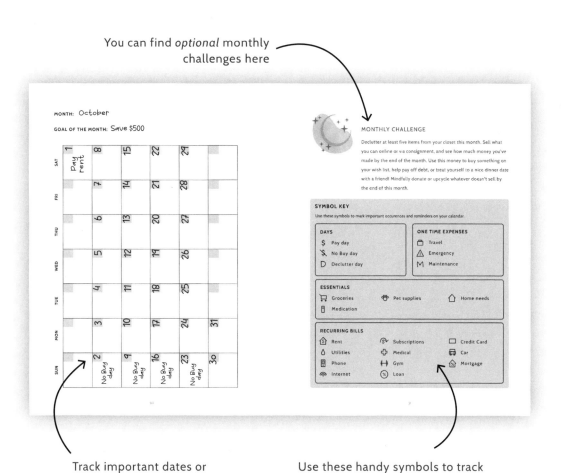

MONTH: October

GOAL OF THE MONTH: Save $500

SUN	MON	TUE	WED	THU	FRI	SAT
						1 Pay rent
2 No Buy day	3	4	5	6	7	8
9 No Buy day	10	11	12	13	14	15
16 No Buy day	17	18	19	20	21	22
23 No Buy day	24	25	26	27	28	29
30	31					

MONTHLY CHALLENGE

Declutter at least five items from your closet this month. Sell what you can online or via consignment, and see how much money you've made by the end of the month. Use this money to buy something on your wish list, help pay off debt, or treat yourself to a nice dinner date with a friend! Mindfully donate or upcycle whatever doesn't sell by the end of this month.

SYMBOL KEY

Use these symbols to mark important occurences and reminders on your calendar.

DAYS
- $ Pay day
- No Buy day
- D Declutter day

ONE TIME EXPENSES
- Travel
- Emergency
- M Maintenance

ESSENTIALS
- Groceries
- Medication
- Pet supplies
- Home needs

RECURRING BILLS
- Rent
- Utilities
- Phone
- Internet
- Subscriptions
- Medical
- Gym
- Loan
- Credit Card
- Car
- Mortgage

Track important dates or Low Buy/No Buy days

Use these handy symbols to track paychecks, recurring bills, and more on your calendars

HOT TIP

It's okay to be unapologetic about where you spend your money in certain cases. Get clear on what you value spending money on and what you don't.

Weekly Check-Ins

Use this template to plan and organize your day-to-day. We've also included a week-in-review so you can reflect back on your week and check in for the days ahead!

WEEK: October 1–6

GOAL OF THE WEEK: Bring lunch to work every day

MON
Rent Due :(

TUE
Dinner w/ Kylee
$$

WED

THU
Dan's B-Day

FRI

SAT

SUN

52

Use the dot grids to write notes, create a key for symbols, or even just doodle.

Remember, habits are built and goals are reached over time. Take
a few minutes to lay out your week, and be sure to weave your
goals into it!

HOW DID THIS WEEK GO?

★★★★☆

CELEBRATE THREE WINS
1. Stuck to my goal
2. Paid rent on time
3. Was able to add to savings

WHAT ARE THREE THINGS I'D IMPROVE?
1. Less buying coffee
2. Less online shopping
3. More thrifting

HOW DID I SUPPORT MY GOAL(S)?
Made lunch the night
before work

Rate your week, celebrate your wins,
and reflect on your goals with
these handy prompts.

Reflections

It's not about perfection, it's about progress. At the end of each month, each quarter, and the year, this journal includes a place to reflect on the progress you've made and the challenges you've faced.

MONTHLY REFLECTION

Use this spread to reflect on your habits and progress from the previous month.

MONTHLY REFLECTION

How closely did I stick to my habits this month?
(Circle one)

1	2	3	4	5
0%	25%	50%	75%	100%

Did I meet my monthly goal(s)? Why or why not?

What went well this month?

What do I want to work on next month?

Use this space to write out, draw, and reflect on your month.

QUARTERLY REFLECTION

Use this spread to review your progress, then refine your process so you can meet your goals.

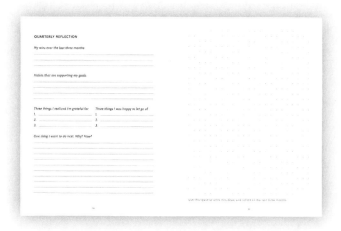

END-OF-YEAR REFLECTION

Use this spread to reflect on your accomplishments, habits, and everything you discovered during your Minimalist-ish year!

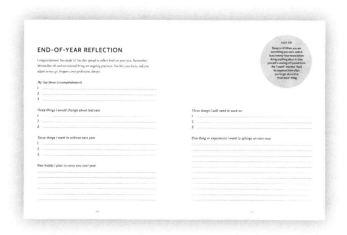

Wish Lists

At the end of this journal, on page 228, you'll find a wish list. A great way to create some distance between yourself and a potential impulse buy is to write it down on a wish list and give yourself a cooling-off period before you actually buy it. Anytime something catches your eye this year, write it down here. When you go back to write down the *next* item on your wish list, review it and see if you even remember what you wrote down in the first place! Cross off what you forgot about, and rinse and repeat. If there's something on your wish list that you really are ready to buy, use your Wish List Item Planner spread to make your plan to buy it with intention!

WISH LIST

BEFORE BUYING, I WILL WAIT (Circle one):

1 DAY | 1 WEEK | 1 MONTH | 1 YEAR

WANT	HOW MUCH	WHY I WANT IT

BEFORE BUYING, I WILL WAIT (Circle one):

1 DAY | 1 WEEK | 1 MONTH | 1 YEAR

WANT	HOW MUCH	WHY I WANT IT

WISH LIST ITEM PLANNING

So you've decided you're ready to buy something on your wish list. Don't let that beautiful thing you're so excited to buy become a burden! Use the Wish List Item Planner on page 230 to plan out how you'll buy your next gem.

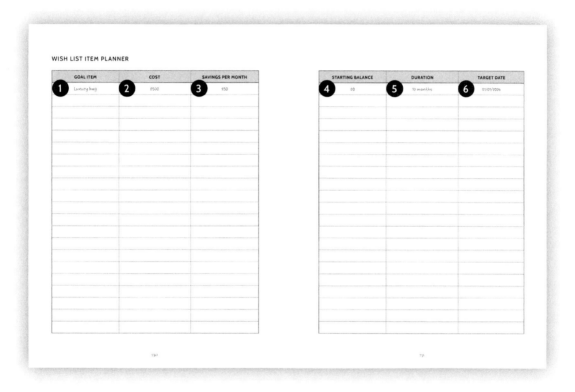

WISH LIST ITEM PLANNER

	GOAL ITEM		COST		SAVINGS PER MONTH
1	Luxury bag	2	$500	3	$50

	STARTING BALANCE		DURATION		TARGET DATE
4	$0	5	10 months	6	01/01/2026

1 List your goal item

2 Log the cost

3 How much you can save per month for this purchase

4 Write your starting balance

5 Calculate how long it will take to save for this expense

$$\frac{\text{Cost - Starting Balance}}{\text{Savings per Month}} = \text{Duration}$$

6 Estimate your target date based on the duration

Inventory Tracking

One of the keys to the Minimalist-ish Method is that we want you to focus less on what comes *next* and more on what's already *here*. After all, a mindset of abundance and gratitude comes from regularly practicing appreciation for what you have *right now*. Use the Inventory Tracker on page 232 to get familiar with all the beautiful things you already own. If you declutter, cross off the items you got rid of. If you buy something new, add it to the inventory. If you're feeling spendy, bookmark this page as a quick, at-a-glance reference to remind you of what you already have.

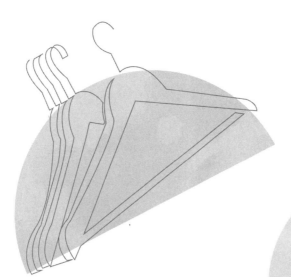

HOT TIP

Keep your space *clutter neutral* by using the one-in, one-out decluttering rule. Every time you want to bring in something new, declutter at least one old thing you're no longer using.

Keep track of specific
categories of items

INVENTORY TRACKER

CATEGORY: Makeup

ITEM	QUANTITY	NOTES
Mascara	5	Use up before buying
Foundation	1	Try to keep inventory to 1
Lipstick	20	Stop buying the same color!
Nail polish	11	Mostly gifted
Eye liner	1	Replace in 2 months
Lip liner	4	I have all I need
Eyeshadow palettes	5	Only buy if you need a specific color
Primer	2	Dewy and matte
Eyeshadow primer	2	White and nude tone
Lip gloss	50	Declutter items older than 1 year
Blush	8	5 cream, 2 powder, 1 serum
Highlighter	2	Warm and cool
Brushes	32	Declutter
BB cream	0	Okay to replace
Eyebrow pencil	1	Use up before buying

232

List items and quantities, along with
notes and reminders

MONTH:

GOAL OF THE MONTH:

SAT					
FRI					
THU					
WED					
TUE					
MON					
SUN					

MONTHLY CHALLENGE

Declutter at least five items from your closet this month. Sell what you can online or via consignment, and see how much money you've made by the end of the month. Use this money to buy something on your wish list, help pay off debt, or treat yourself to a nice dinner date with a friend! Mindfully donate or upcycle whatever doesn't sell by the end of this month.

SYMBOL KEY

Use these symbols to mark important occurrences and reminders on your calendar.

DAYS

- $ Payday
- $ No Buy day
- D Declutter day

ONETIME EXPENSES

- 🧳 Travel
- ⚠ Emergency
- M Maintenance

ESSENTIALS

- 🛒 Groceries
- 💊 Medication
- 🐾 Pet supplies
- 🏠 Home needs

RECURRING BILLS

- 🏠 Rent
- 💧 Utilities
- 📱 Phone
- 📶 Internet
- 💲 Subscriptions
- ✚ Medical
- ╟╢ Gym
- % Loan
- ▭ Credit Card
- 🚗 Car
- % Mortgage

WEEK:

GOAL OF THE WEEK:

MON
TUE
WED
THU
FRI
SAT
SUN

HOW DID THIS WEEK GO?

☆ ☆ ☆ ☆ ☆

CELEBRATE THREE WINS

1. _____
2. _____
3. _____

WHAT ARE THREE THINGS I'D IMPROVE?

1. _____
2. _____
3. _____

HOW DID I SUPPORT MY GOAL(S)?

_____
_____
_____
_____
_____
_____
_____
_____
_____
_____
_____
_____

WEEK:

GOAL OF THE WEEK:

MON

TUE

WED

THU

FRI

SAT

SUN

HOW DID THIS WEEK GO?

☆ ☆ ☆ ☆ ☆

CELEBRATE THREE WINS

1. _____
2. _____
3. _____

WHAT ARE THREE THINGS I'D IMPROVE?

1. _____
2. _____
3. _____

HOW DID I SUPPORT MY GOAL(S)?

_____
_____
_____
_____
_____
_____
_____
_____
_____
_____
_____
_____
_____
_____

WEEK:

GOAL OF THE WEEK:

MON

TUE

WED

THU

FRI

SAT

SUN

HOW DID THIS WEEK GO?

☆ ☆ ☆ ☆ ☆

CELEBRATE THREE WINS

1. _____
2. _____
3. _____

WHAT ARE THREE THINGS I'D IMPROVE?

1. _____
2. _____
3. _____

HOW DID I SUPPORT MY GOAL(S)?

_____
_____
_____
_____
_____
_____
_____
_____
_____
_____
_____
_____
_____
_____
_____

WEEK:

GOAL OF THE WEEK:

MON
TUE
WED
THU
FRI
SAT
SUN

HOW DID THIS WEEK GO?

☆ ☆ ☆ ☆ ☆

CELEBRATE THREE WINS

1. _____
2. _____
3. _____

WHAT ARE THREE THINGS I'D IMPROVE?

1. _____
2. _____
3. _____

HOW DID I SUPPORT MY GOAL(S)?

_____
_____
_____
_____
_____
_____
_____
_____
_____
_____
_____
_____
_____

WEEK:

GOAL OF THE WEEK:

MON
TUE
WED
THU
FRI
SAT
SUN

HOW DID THIS WEEK GO?

☆ ☆ ☆ ☆ ☆

CELEBRATE THREE WINS

1. _____
2. _____
3. _____

WHAT ARE THREE THINGS I'D IMPROVE?

1. _____
2. _____
3. _____

HOW DID I SUPPORT MY GOAL(S)?

_____
_____
_____
_____
_____
_____
_____
_____
_____
_____
_____
_____
_____
_____

MONTHLY REFLECTION

How closely did I stick to my habits this month?
(Circle one)

1	2	3	4	5
0%	25%	50%	75%	100%

Did I meet my monthly goal(s)? Why or why not?

_____

_____

_____

_____

_____

What went well this month?

_____

_____

_____

_____

_____

What do I want to work on next month?

_____

_____

_____

_____

_____

Use this space to write out, draw, and reflect on your month.

MONTH:

GOAL OF THE MONTH:

SAT					
FRI					
THU					
WED					
TUE					
MON					
SUN					

MONTHLY CHALLENGE

Choose at least one item from your closet that you never wear but haven't brought yourself to declutter yet. Style three outfits using the item, and take a selfie in each one. Reflect on how doing this felt. Did you feel excited about the outfits, or did they feel "off"? Are you going to keep the item, or did you realize it's not for you? Sell it or donate it if not!

SYMBOL KEY

Use these symbols to mark important occurrences and reminders on your calendar.

DAYS

$ Payday

$̸   No Buy day

D   Declutter day

ONETIME EXPENSES

  Travel

⚠   Emergency

M   Maintenance

ESSENTIALS

🛒   Groceries   🐾   Pet supplies   ⌂   Home needs

💊   Medication

RECURRING BILLS

🏠$ Rent $↴   Subscriptions   ▭   Credit Card

💧   Utilities   ✚   Medical   🚘   Car

📱   Phone   ⊢⊣   Gym   🏠%   Mortgage

📶   Internet   %   Loan

WEEK:

GOAL OF THE WEEK:

MON

TUE

WED

THU

FRI

SAT

SUN

HOW DID THIS WEEK GO?

☆ ☆ ☆ ☆ ☆

CELEBRATE THREE WINS

1. _____
2. _____
3. _____

WHAT ARE THREE THINGS I'D IMPROVE?

1. _____
2. _____
3. _____

HOW DID I SUPPORT MY GOAL(S)?

_____
_____
_____
_____
_____
_____
_____
_____
_____
_____
_____
_____
_____
_____

WEEK:

GOAL OF THE WEEK:

MON
TUE
WED
THU
FRI
SAT
SUN

HOW DID THIS WEEK GO?

☆ ☆ ☆ ☆ ☆

CELEBRATE THREE WINS

1. _____
2. _____
3. _____

WHAT ARE THREE THINGS I'D IMPROVE?

1. _____
2. _____
3. _____

HOW DID I SUPPORT MY GOAL(S)?

_____
_____
_____
_____
_____
_____
_____
_____
_____
_____
_____
_____
_____

WEEK:

GOAL OF THE WEEK:

MON

TUE

WED

THU

FRI

SAT

SUN

HOW DID THIS WEEK GO?

☆ ☆ ☆ ☆ ☆

CELEBRATE THREE WINS

1. _____
2. _____
3. _____

WHAT ARE THREE THINGS I'D IMPROVE?

1. _____
2. _____
3. _____

HOW DID I SUPPORT MY GOAL(S)?

_____
_____
_____
_____
_____
_____
_____
_____
_____
_____
_____
_____
_____

WEEK:

GOAL OF THE WEEK:

MON

TUE

WED

THU

FRI

SAT

SUN

HOW DID THIS WEEK GO?

☆ ☆ ☆ ☆ ☆

CELEBRATE THREE WINS

1. _____
2. _____
3. _____

WHAT ARE THREE THINGS I'D IMPROVE?

1. _____
2. _____
3. _____

HOW DID I SUPPORT MY GOAL(S)?

_____
_____
_____
_____
_____
_____
_____
_____
_____
_____
_____
_____
_____

WEEK:

GOAL OF THE WEEK:

MON

TUE

WED

THU

FRI

SAT

SUN

HOW DID THIS WEEK GO?

☆ ☆ ☆ ☆ ☆

CELEBRATE THREE WINS

1. _____
2. _____
3. _____

WHAT ARE THREE THINGS I'D IMPROVE?

1. _____
2. _____
3. _____

HOW DID I SUPPORT MY GOAL(S)?

_____
_____
_____
_____
_____
_____
_____
_____
_____
_____
_____
_____

MONTHLY REFLECTION

How closely did I stick to my habits this month?
(Circle one)

1	2	3	4	5
0%	25%	50%	75%	100%

Did I meet my monthly goal(s)? Why or why not?

_____

_____

_____

_____

_____

What went well this month?

_____

_____

_____

_____

_____

What do I want to work on next month?

_____

_____

_____

_____

_____

_____

Use this space to write out, draw, and reflect on your month.

MONTH:

GOAL OF THE MONTH:

SAT					
FRI					
THU					
WED					
TUE					
MON					
SUN					

MONTHLY CHALLENGE

Declutter your makeup stash! Take some time this month to audit and edit your makeup collection. Is anything expired? Are there any colors you no longer wear? Is anything feeling chalky, patchy, or dry? Once your collection is edited, create at least one makeup look using the items you've decided to keep. Take a selfie, since you're feeling glam! Consider donating any unopened, unexpired items to your local women's shelter.

SYMBOL KEY

Use these symbols to mark important occurrences and reminders on your calendar.

DAYS

$ Payday

$ No Buy day

D Declutter day

ONETIME EXPENSES

Travel

Emergency

M Maintenance

ESSENTIALS

Groceries

Medication

Pet supplies

Home needs

RECURRING BILLS

Rent

Utilities

Phone

Internet

Subscriptions

Medical

Gym

Loan

Credit Card

Car

Mortgage

WEEK:

GOAL OF THE WEEK:

MON
TUE
WED
THU
FRI
SAT
SUN

HOW DID THIS WEEK GO?

☆ ☆ ☆ ☆ ☆

CELEBRATE THREE WINS

1. _____
2. _____
3. _____

WHAT ARE THREE THINGS I'D IMPROVE?

1. _____
2. _____
3. _____

HOW DID I SUPPORT MY GOAL(S)?

_____
_____
_____
_____
_____
_____
_____
_____
_____
_____
_____
_____
_____

WEEK:

GOAL OF THE WEEK:

MON
TUE
WED
THU
FRI
SAT
SUN

HOW DID THIS WEEK GO?

☆ ☆ ☆ ☆ ☆

CELEBRATE THREE WINS

1. _____
2. _____
3. _____

WHAT ARE THREE THINGS I'D IMPROVE?

1. _____
2. _____
3. _____

HOW DID I SUPPORT MY GOAL(S)?

_____
_____
_____
_____
_____
_____
_____
_____
_____
_____
_____
_____
_____
_____

WEEK:

GOAL OF THE WEEK:

MON

TUE

WED

THU

FRI

SAT

SUN

HOW DID THIS WEEK GO?

☆ ☆ ☆ ☆ ☆

CELEBRATE THREE WINS

1. _____
2. _____
3. _____

WHAT ARE THREE THINGS I'D IMPROVE?

1. _____
2. _____
3. _____

HOW DID I SUPPORT MY GOAL(S)?

_____
_____
_____
_____
_____
_____
_____
_____
_____
_____
_____
_____
_____
_____

WEEK:

GOAL OF THE WEEK:

MON
TUE
WED
THU
FRI
SAT
SUN

HOW DID THIS WEEK GO?

☆ ☆ ☆ ☆ ☆

CELEBRATE THREE WINS

1. _____
2. _____
3. _____

WHAT ARE THREE THINGS I'D IMPROVE?

1. _____
2. _____
3. _____

HOW DID I SUPPORT MY GOAL(S)?

_____
_____
_____
_____
_____
_____
_____
_____
_____
_____
_____
_____

WEEK:

GOAL OF THE WEEK:

MON

TUE

WED

THU

FRI

SAT

SUN

HOW DID THIS WEEK GO?

☆ ☆ ☆ ☆ ☆

CELEBRATE THREE WINS

1. _____
2. _____
3. _____

WHAT ARE THREE THINGS I'D IMPROVE?

1. _____
2. _____
3. _____

HOW DID I SUPPORT MY GOAL(S)?

_____
_____
_____
_____
_____
_____
_____
_____
_____
_____
_____
_____
_____

MONTHLY REFLECTION

How closely did I stick to my habits this month?
(Circle one)

1	2	3	4	5
0%	25%	50%	75%	100%

Did I meet my monthly goal(s)? Why or why not?

_____

_____

_____

_____

_____

What went well this month?

_____

_____

_____

_____

_____

What do I want to work on next month?

_____

_____

_____

_____

_____

Use this space to write out, draw, and reflect on your month.

QUARTERLY REFLECTION

My wins over the last three months

_____

_____

_____

Habits that are supporting my goals

_____

_____

_____

_____

Three things I realized I'm grateful for

1. _____

2. _____

3. _____

Three things I was happy to let go of

1. _____

2. _____

3. _____

One thing I want to do next. Why? How?

_____

_____

_____

_____

_____

_____

_____

_____

_____

Use this space to write out, draw, and reflect on the last three months.

MONTH:

GOAL OF THE MONTH:

SAT					
FRI					
THU					
WED					
TUE					
MON					
SUN					

MONTHLY CHALLENGE

Save an extra $200 this month. Review your monthly expenses and see what you can cut down on to meet your goal. You can do things like calling your bank to see if you're paying any unnecessary fees, canceling subscriptions you don't use, selling clothes you no longer wear, or preparing your lunches at home every day to cut costs. If you have a side hustle, see if you can get extra clients this month to increase your income.

SYMBOL KEY

Use these symbols to mark important occurrences and reminders on your calendar.

DAYS

$ Payday

$ No Buy day

D Declutter day

ONETIME EXPENSES

Travel

⚠ Emergency

M Maintenance

ESSENTIALS

🛒 Groceries

🐾 Pet supplies

⌂ Home needs

Medication

RECURRING BILLS

Rent

Utilities

Phone

Internet

Subscriptions

Medical

Gym

% Loan

Credit Card

Car

% Mortgage

WEEK:

GOAL OF THE WEEK:

MON

TUE

WED

THU

FRI

SAT

SUN

HOW DID THIS WEEK GO?

☆ ☆ ☆ ☆ ☆

CELEBRATE THREE WINS

1. _____
2. _____
3. _____

WHAT ARE THREE THINGS I'D IMPROVE?

1. _____
2. _____
3. _____

HOW DID I SUPPORT MY GOAL(S)?

_____
_____
_____
_____
_____
_____
_____
_____
_____
_____
_____
_____
_____

WEEK:

GOAL OF THE WEEK:

MON

TUE

WED

THU

FRI

SAT

SUN

HOW DID THIS WEEK GO?

☆ ☆ ☆ ☆ ☆

CELEBRATE THREE WINS

1. _____
2. _____
3. _____

WHAT ARE THREE THINGS I'D IMPROVE?

1. _____
2. _____
3. _____

HOW DID I SUPPORT MY GOAL(S)?

_____
_____
_____
_____
_____
_____
_____
_____
_____
_____
_____
_____
_____
_____

WEEK:

GOAL OF THE WEEK:

MON

TUE

WED

THU

FRI

SAT

SUN

HOW DID THIS WEEK GO?

☆ ☆ ☆ ☆ ☆

CELEBRATE THREE WINS

1. _____
2. _____
3. _____

WHAT ARE THREE THINGS I'D IMPROVE?

1. _____
2. _____
3. _____

HOW DID I SUPPORT MY GOAL(S)?

_____
_____
_____
_____
_____
_____
_____
_____
_____
_____
_____
_____
_____
_____
_____

WEEK:

GOAL OF THE WEEK:

MON
TUE
WED
THU
FRI
SAT
SUN

HOW DID THIS WEEK GO?

☆ ☆ ☆ ☆ ☆

CELEBRATE THREE WINS

1. _____
2. _____
3. _____

WHAT ARE THREE THINGS I'D IMPROVE?

1. _____
2. _____
3. _____

HOW DID I SUPPORT MY GOAL(S)?

_____
_____
_____
_____
_____
_____
_____
_____
_____
_____
_____
_____

WEEK:

GOAL OF THE WEEK:

MON
TUE
WED
THU
FRI
SAT
SUN

HOW DID THIS WEEK GO?

☆ ☆ ☆ ☆ ☆

CELEBRATE THREE WINS

1. _____
2. _____
3. _____

WHAT ARE THREE THINGS I'D IMPROVE?

1. _____
2. _____
3. _____

HOW DID I SUPPORT MY GOAL(S)?

_____
_____
_____
_____
_____
_____
_____
_____
_____
_____
_____
_____
_____

MONTHLY REFLECTION

How closely did I stick to my habits this month?
(Circle one)

1	2	3	4	5
0%	25%	50%	75%	100%

Did I meet my monthly goal(s)? Why or why not?

_____

_____

_____

_____

_____

What went well this month?

_____

_____

_____

_____

_____

What do I want to work on next month?

_____

_____

_____

_____

_____

Use this space to write out, draw, and reflect on your month.

MONTH:

GOAL OF THE MONTH:

SAT					
FRI					
THU					
WED					
TUE					
MON					
SUN					

MONTHLY CHALLENGE

Plan a guilt-free rest day. Put your phone on Do Not Disturb and stay off social media. Wear your comfiest loungewear. Light a candle. Put on your favorite show and get your snacks ready. No chores, no tidying, no to-do list. Enjoy your intentional Do Nothing day!

SYMBOL KEY

Use these symbols to mark important occurrences and reminders on your calendar.

DAYS

- $ Payday
- $ No Buy day
- D   Declutter day

ONETIME EXPENSES

- Travel
- Emergency
- M   Maintenance

ESSENTIALS

- Groceries
- Medication
- Pet supplies
- Home needs

RECURRING BILLS

- Rent
- Utilities
- Phone
- Internet
- Subscriptions
- Medical
- Gym
- Loan
- Credit Card
- Car
- Mortgage

WEEK:

GOAL OF THE WEEK:

MON

TUE

WED

THU

FRI

SAT

SUN

HOW DID THIS WEEK GO?

☆ ☆ ☆ ☆ ☆

CELEBRATE THREE WINS

1. _____
2. _____
3. _____

WHAT ARE THREE THINGS I'D IMPROVE?

1. _____
2. _____
3. _____

HOW DID I SUPPORT MY GOAL(S)?

_____
_____
_____
_____
_____
_____
_____
_____
_____
_____
_____
_____
_____
_____
_____
_____

WEEK:

GOAL OF THE WEEK:

MON
TUE
WED
THU
FRI
SAT
SUN

HOW DID THIS WEEK GO?

☆ ☆ ☆ ☆ ☆

CELEBRATE THREE WINS

1. _____
2. _____
3. _____

WHAT ARE THREE THINGS I'D IMPROVE?

1. _____
2. _____
3. _____

HOW DID I SUPPORT MY GOAL(S)?

_____
_____
_____
_____
_____
_____
_____
_____
_____
_____
_____
_____
_____
_____

WEEK:

GOAL OF THE WEEK:

MON
TUE
WED
THU
FRI
SAT
SUN

HOW DID THIS WEEK GO?

☆ ☆ ☆ ☆ ☆

CELEBRATE THREE WINS

1. _____
2. _____
3. _____

WHAT ARE THREE THINGS I'D IMPROVE?

1. _____
2. _____
3. _____

HOW DID I SUPPORT MY GOAL(S)?

_____
_____
_____
_____
_____
_____
_____
_____
_____
_____
_____
_____
_____

WEEK:

GOAL OF THE WEEK:

MON
TUE
WED
THU
FRI
SAT
SUN

HOW DID THIS WEEK GO?

☆ ☆ ☆ ☆ ☆

CELEBRATE THREE WINS

1. _____
2. _____
3. _____

WHAT ARE THREE THINGS I'D IMPROVE?

1. _____
2. _____
3. _____

HOW DID I SUPPORT MY GOAL(S)?

_____
_____
_____
_____
_____
_____
_____
_____
_____
_____
_____
_____
_____

WEEK:

GOAL OF THE WEEK:

MON

TUE

WED

THU

FRI

SAT

SUN

HOW DID THIS WEEK GO?

☆ ☆ ☆ ☆ ☆

CELEBRATE THREE WINS

1. _____
2. _____
3. _____

WHAT ARE THREE THINGS I'D IMPROVE?

1. _____
2. _____
3. _____

HOW DID I SUPPORT MY GOAL(S)?

_____
_____
_____
_____
_____
_____
_____
_____
_____
_____
_____
_____
_____
_____

MONTHLY REFLECTION

How closely did I stick to my habits this month?
(Circle one)

1	2	3	4	5
0%	25%	50%	75%	100%

Did I meet my monthly goal(s)? Why or why not?

_____

_____

_____

_____

_____

What went well this month?

_____

_____

_____

_____

_____

What do I want to work on next month?

_____

_____

_____

_____

_____

_____

Use this space to write out, draw, and reflect on your month.

MONTH:

GOAL OF THE MONTH:

	SUN	MON	TUE	WED	THU	FRI	SAT

MONTHLY CHALLENGE

Read a book about money or listen to at least one personal-finance podcast this month. Write down one to three key takeaways you learned. Learning more about money is a great way to help reframe your spending habits.

SYMBOL KEY

Use these symbols to mark important occurrences and reminders on your calendar.

DAYS

$ Payday

$ No Buy day

D Declutter day

ONETIME EXPENSES

Travel

Emergency

M Maintenance

ESSENTIALS

Groceries

Medication

Pet supplies

Home needs

RECURRING BILLS

Rent

Utilities

Phone

Internet

Subscriptions

Medical

Gym

Loan

Credit Card

Car

Mortgage

WEEK:

GOAL OF THE WEEK:

MON

TUE

WED

THU

FRI

SAT

SUN

HOW DID THIS WEEK GO?

☆ ☆ ☆ ☆ ☆

CELEBRATE THREE WINS

1. _____
2. _____
3. _____

WHAT ARE THREE THINGS I'D IMPROVE?

1. _____
2. _____
3. _____

HOW DID I SUPPORT MY GOAL(S)?

_____
_____
_____
_____
_____
_____
_____
_____
_____
_____
_____
_____

WEEK:

GOAL OF THE WEEK:

MON
TUE
WED
THU
FRI
SAT
SUN

HOW DID THIS WEEK GO?

☆ ☆ ☆ ☆ ☆

CELEBRATE THREE WINS

1. _____
2. _____
3. _____

WHAT ARE THREE THINGS I'D IMPROVE?

1. _____
2. _____
3. _____

HOW DID I SUPPORT MY GOAL(S)?

_____
_____
_____
_____
_____
_____
_____
_____
_____
_____
_____
_____

WEEK:

GOAL OF THE WEEK:

MON
TUE
WED
THU
FRI
SAT
SUN

HOW DID THIS WEEK GO?

☆ ☆ ☆ ☆ ☆

CELEBRATE THREE WINS

1. _____
2. _____
3. _____

WHAT ARE THREE THINGS I'D IMPROVE?

1. _____
2. _____
3. _____

HOW DID I SUPPORT MY GOAL(S)?

_____
_____
_____
_____
_____
_____
_____
_____
_____
_____
_____
_____
_____
_____

WEEK:

GOAL OF THE WEEK:

MON
TUE
WED
THU
FRI
SAT
SUN

HOW DID THIS WEEK GO?

☆ ☆ ☆ ☆ ☆

CELEBRATE THREE WINS

1. _____
2. _____
3. _____

WHAT ARE THREE THINGS I'D IMPROVE?

1. _____
2. _____
3. _____

HOW DID I SUPPORT MY GOAL(S)?

_____
_____
_____
_____
_____
_____
_____
_____
_____
_____
_____
_____

WEEK:

GOAL OF THE WEEK:

MON

TUE

WED

THU

FRI

SAT

SUN

HOW DID THIS WEEK GO?

☆ ☆ ☆ ☆ ☆

CELEBRATE THREE WINS

1. _____
2. _____
3. _____

WHAT ARE THREE THINGS I'D IMPROVE?

1. _____
2. _____
3. _____

HOW DID I SUPPORT MY GOAL(S)?

_____
_____
_____
_____
_____
_____
_____
_____
_____
_____
_____
_____
_____

MONTHLY REFLECTION

How closely did I stick to my habits this month?
(*Circle one*)

1	2	3	4	5
0%	25%	50%	75%	100%

Did I meet my monthly goal(s)? Why or why not?

_____

_____

_____

_____

_____

What went well this month?

_____

_____

_____

_____

_____

What do I want to work on next month?

_____

_____

_____

_____

_____

_____

Use this space to write out, draw, and reflect on your month.

QUARTERLY REFLECTION

My wins over the last three months

_____

_____

_____

Habits that are supporting my goals

_____

_____

_____

_____

Three things I realized I'm grateful for

1. _____

2. _____

3. _____

Three things I was happy to let go of

1. _____

2. _____

3. _____

One thing I want to do next. Why? How?

_____

_____

_____

_____

_____

_____

_____

_____

_____

Use this space to write out, draw, and reflect on the last three months.

MONTH:

GOAL OF THE MONTH:

	SAT	FRI	THU	WED	TUE	MON	SUN

MONTHLY CHALLENGE

Find your Personal Style Uniform. Discover the outfit combinations you wear most often by taking an outfit-of-the-day selfie every day for one week. Choose three or four of your favorite outfits, and write down what they have in common. Do you like to wear separates, like pants and a T-shirt? Or are you more of a dress person? Do you wear mostly sneakers or loafers? Write down your go-to outfit combinations, and see how easy it is to get dressed after that!

SYMBOL KEY

Use these symbols to mark important occurrences and reminders on your calendar.

DAYS

$ Payday

$ No Buy day

D   Declutter day

ONETIME EXPENSES

   Travel

⚠   Emergency

M   Maintenance

ESSENTIALS

🛒   Groceries   🐾   Pet supplies   🏠   Home needs

💊   Medication

RECURRING BILLS

🏠   Rent $↻   Subscriptions   💳   Credit Card

💧   Utilities   ✚   Medical   🚗   Car

📱   Phone   Ⱶ   Gym   %   Mortgage

📶   Internet   %   Loan

WEEK:

GOAL OF THE WEEK:

MON

TUE

WED

THU

FRI

SAT

SUN

HOW DID THIS WEEK GO?

☆ ☆ ☆ ☆ ☆

CELEBRATE THREE WINS

1. _____

2. _____

3. _____

WHAT ARE THREE THINGS I'D IMPROVE?

1. _____

2. _____

3. _____

HOW DID I SUPPORT MY GOAL(S)?

_____

_____

_____

_____

_____

_____

_____

_____

_____

_____

_____

_____

_____

_____

WEEK:

GOAL OF THE WEEK:

MON
TUE
WED
THU
FRI
SAT
SUN

HOW DID THIS WEEK GO?

☆ ☆ ☆ ☆ ☆

CELEBRATE THREE WINS

1. _____
2. _____
3. _____

WHAT ARE THREE THINGS I'D IMPROVE?

1. _____
2. _____
3. _____

HOW DID I SUPPORT MY GOAL(S)?

_____
_____
_____
_____
_____
_____
_____
_____
_____
_____
_____
_____
_____
_____

WEEK:

GOAL OF THE WEEK:

MON

TUE

WED

THU

FRI

SAT

SUN

HOW DID THIS WEEK GO?

☆ ☆ ☆ ☆ ☆

CELEBRATE THREE WINS

1. _____
2. _____
3. _____

WHAT ARE THREE THINGS I'D IMPROVE?

1. _____
2. _____
3. _____

HOW DID I SUPPORT MY GOAL(S)?

_____
_____
_____
_____
_____
_____
_____
_____
_____
_____
_____
_____
_____

WEEK:

GOAL OF THE WEEK:

MON

TUE

WED

THU

FRI

SAT

SUN

HOW DID THIS WEEK GO?

☆ ☆ ☆ ☆ ☆

CELEBRATE THREE WINS

1. _____
2. _____
3. _____

WHAT ARE THREE THINGS I'D IMPROVE?

1. _____
2. _____
3. _____

HOW DID I SUPPORT MY GOAL(S)?

_____
_____
_____
_____
_____
_____
_____
_____
_____
_____
_____
_____
_____

WEEK:

GOAL OF THE WEEK:

MON
TUE
WED
THU
FRI
SAT
SUN

HOW DID THIS WEEK GO?

☆ ☆ ☆ ☆ ☆

CELEBRATE THREE WINS

1. _____
2. _____
3. _____

WHAT ARE THREE THINGS I'D IMPROVE?

1. _____
2. _____
3. _____

HOW DID I SUPPORT MY GOAL(S)?

_____
_____
_____
_____
_____
_____
_____
_____
_____
_____
_____
_____
_____

MONTHLY REFLECTION

How closely did I stick to my habits this month?
(Circle one)

1	2	3	4	5
0%	25%	50%	75%	100%

Did I meet my monthly goal(s)? Why or why not?

_____

_____

_____

_____

_____

What went well this month?

_____

_____

_____

_____

_____

What do I want to work on next month?

_____

_____

_____

_____

_____

_____

Use this space to write out, draw, and reflect on your month.

MONTH:

GOAL OF THE MONTH:

	SAT	FRI	THU	WED	TUE	MON	SUN

MONTHLY CHALLENGE

Re-create three to five outfits from your social media saves or your online mood board using *only* pieces you already own. See what new go-to looks you can incorporate into your regular rotation, and make your old clothes feel new again!

SYMBOL KEY

Use these symbols to mark important occurrences and reminders on your calendar.

DAYS

$ Payday

✗ No Buy day

D Declutter day

ONETIME EXPENSES

▯ Travel

⚠ Emergency

M Maintenance

ESSENTIALS

🛒 Groceries

🐾 Pet supplies

⌂ Home needs

▯ Medication

RECURRING BILLS

⌂$ Rent

⟳$ Subscriptions

▭ Credit Card

◊ Utilities

✚ Medical

🚃 Car

▯ Phone

⊦⊣ Gym

⌂% Mortgage

📶 Internet

% Loan

WEEK:

GOAL OF THE WEEK:

MON
TUE
WED
THU
FRI
SAT
SUN

HOW DID THIS WEEK GO?

☆ ☆ ☆ ☆ ☆

CELEBRATE THREE WINS

1. _____
2. _____
3. _____

WHAT ARE THREE THINGS I'D IMPROVE?

1. _____
2. _____
3. _____

HOW DID I SUPPORT MY GOAL(S)?

_____
_____
_____
_____
_____
_____
_____
_____
_____
_____
_____
_____
_____
_____

WEEK:

GOAL OF THE WEEK:

MON

TUE

WED

THU

FRI

SAT

SUN

HOW DID THIS WEEK GO?

☆ ☆ ☆ ☆ ☆

CELEBRATE THREE WINS

1. _____
2. _____
3. _____

WHAT ARE THREE THINGS I'D IMPROVE?

1. _____
2. _____
3. _____

HOW DID I SUPPORT MY GOAL(S)?

_____
_____
_____
_____
_____
_____
_____
_____
_____
_____
_____
_____
_____
_____

WEEK:

GOAL OF THE WEEK:

MON
TUE
WED
THU
FRI
SAT
SUN

HOW DID THIS WEEK GO?

☆ ☆ ☆ ☆ ☆

CELEBRATE THREE WINS

1. _____
2. _____
3. _____

WHAT ARE THREE THINGS I'D IMPROVE?

1. _____
2. _____
3. _____

HOW DID I SUPPORT MY GOAL(S)?

_____
_____
_____
_____
_____
_____
_____
_____
_____
_____
_____
_____
_____
_____

WEEK:

GOAL OF THE WEEK:

MON

TUE

WED

THU

FRI

SAT

SUN

HOW DID THIS WEEK GO?

☆ ☆ ☆ ☆ ☆

CELEBRATE THREE WINS

1. _____
2. _____
3. _____

WHAT ARE THREE THINGS I'D IMPROVE?

1. _____
2. _____
3. _____

HOW DID I SUPPORT MY GOAL(S)?

_____
_____
_____
_____
_____
_____
_____
_____
_____
_____
_____
_____
_____
_____

WEEK:

GOAL OF THE WEEK:

MON
TUE
WED
THU
FRI
SAT
SUN

HOW DID THIS WEEK GO?

☆ ☆ ☆ ☆ ☆

CELEBRATE THREE WINS

1. _____

2. _____

3. _____

WHAT ARE THREE THINGS I'D IMPROVE?

1. _____

2. _____

3. _____

HOW DID I SUPPORT MY GOAL(S)?

_____

_____

_____

_____

_____

_____

_____

_____

_____

_____

_____

_____

_____

MONTHLY REFLECTION

How closely did I stick to my habits this month?
(Circle one)

1	2	3	4	5
0%	25%	50%	75%	100%

Did I meet my monthly goal(s)? Why or why not?

_____

_____

_____

_____

_____

What went well this month?

_____

_____

_____

_____

_____

What do I want to work on next month?

_____

_____

_____

_____

_____

_____

Use this space to write out, draw, and reflect on your month.

MONTH:

GOAL OF THE MONTH:

	SUN	MON	TUE	WED	THU	FRI	SAT

MONTHLY CHALLENGE

Clear the digital clutter! Unsubscribe from retailer email alerts and delete shopping apps from your phone. If you don't know it's on sale, are you really missing anything? Bonus: unfollow influencers on social media who make you feel spendy or bad about yourself.

SYMBOL KEY

Use these symbols to mark important occurrences and reminders on your calendar.

DAYS

$ Payday

$\not{S}$ No Buy day

D   Declutter day

ONETIME EXPENSES

▯   Travel

⚠   Emergency

M   Maintenance

ESSENTIALS

🛒   Groceries   🐾   Pet supplies   ⌂   Home needs

▯   Medication

RECURRING BILLS

⌂$ Rent   (S↘)   Subscriptions   ▭   Credit Card

◊   Utilities   ✚   Medical   🚗   Car

▯   Phone   ⊢⊣   Gym   ⌂%   Mortgage

📶   Internet   %   Loan

WEEK:

GOAL OF THE WEEK:

MON
TUE
WED
THU
FRI
SAT
SUN

HOW DID THIS WEEK GO?

☆ ☆ ☆ ☆ ☆

CELEBRATE THREE WINS

1. _____
2. _____
3. _____

WHAT ARE THREE THINGS I'D IMPROVE?

1. _____
2. _____
3. _____

HOW DID I SUPPORT MY GOAL(S)?

_____
_____
_____
_____
_____
_____
_____
_____
_____
_____
_____
_____

WEEK:

GOAL OF THE WEEK:

MON
TUE
WED
THU
FRI
SAT
SUN

HOW DID THIS WEEK GO?

☆ ☆ ☆ ☆ ☆

CELEBRATE THREE WINS

1. _____
2. _____
3. _____

WHAT ARE THREE THINGS I'D IMPROVE?

1. _____
2. _____
3. _____

HOW DID I SUPPORT MY GOAL(S)?

_____
_____
_____
_____
_____
_____
_____
_____
_____
_____
_____
_____
_____

WEEK:

GOAL OF THE WEEK:

MON
TUE
WED
THU
FRI
SAT
SUN

HOW DID THIS WEEK GO?

☆ ☆ ☆ ☆ ☆

CELEBRATE THREE WINS

1. _____
2. _____
3. _____

WHAT ARE THREE THINGS I'D IMPROVE?

1. _____
2. _____
3. _____

HOW DID I SUPPORT MY GOAL(S)?

_____
_____
_____
_____
_____
_____
_____
_____
_____
_____
_____
_____
_____

WEEK:

GOAL OF THE WEEK:

MON
TUE
WED
THU
FRI
SAT
SUN

HOW DID THIS WEEK GO?

☆ ☆ ☆ ☆ ☆

CELEBRATE THREE WINS

1. _____
2. _____
3. _____

WHAT ARE THREE THINGS I'D IMPROVE?

1. _____
2. _____
3. _____

HOW DID I SUPPORT MY GOAL(S)?

_____
_____
_____
_____
_____
_____
_____
_____
_____
_____
_____
_____

WEEK:

GOAL OF THE WEEK:

MON
TUE
WED
THU
FRI
SAT
SUN

HOW DID THIS WEEK GO?

☆ ☆ ☆ ☆ ☆

CELEBRATE THREE WINS

1. _____
2. _____
3. _____

WHAT ARE THREE THINGS I'D IMPROVE?

1. _____
2. _____
3. _____

HOW DID I SUPPORT MY GOAL(S)?

_____
_____
_____
_____
_____
_____
_____
_____
_____
_____
_____
_____
_____
_____

MONTHLY REFLECTION

How closely did I stick to my habits this month?
(Circle one)

1	2	3	4	5
0%	25%	50%	75%	100%

Did I meet my monthly goal(s)? Why or why not?

_____

_____

_____

_____

_____

What went well this month?

_____

_____

_____

_____

_____

What do I want to work on next month?

_____

_____

_____

_____

_____

_____

Use this space to write out, draw, and reflect on your month.

QUARTERLY REFLECTION

My wins over the last three months

_____

_____

_____

Habits that are supporting my goals

_____

_____

_____

_____

Three things I realized I'm grateful for

1. _____

2. _____

3. _____

Three things I was happy to let go of

1. _____

2. _____

3. _____

One thing I want to do next. Why? How?

_____

_____

_____

_____

_____

_____

_____

_____

Use this space to write out, draw, and reflect on the last three months.

MONTH:

GOAL OF THE MONTH:

SAT					
FRI					
THU					
WED					
TUE					
MON					
SUN					

MONTHLY CHALLENGE

Try a mini capsule wardrobe challenge! Take seven to ten items from your wardrobe and style only these items for the next week! See how many new outfits you can come up with. Don't forget to take selfies!

SYMBOL KEY

Use these symbols to mark important occurrences and reminders on your calendar.

DAYS

$ Payday

$ No Buy day

D   Declutter day

ONETIME EXPENSES

📁   Travel

⚠   Emergency

M   Maintenance

ESSENTIALS

🛒   Groceries   🐾   Pet supplies   ⌂   Home needs

💊   Medication

RECURRING BILLS

🏠   Rent $ Subscriptions   ▭   Credit Card

💧   Utilities   ✚   Medical   🚗   Car

📱   Phone   🏋   Gym   🏠   Mortgage

📶   Internet   %   Loan

WEEK:

GOAL OF THE WEEK:

MON
TUE
WED
THU
FRI
SAT
SUN

HOW DID THIS WEEK GO?

☆ ☆ ☆ ☆ ☆

CELEBRATE THREE WINS

1. _____
2. _____
3. _____

WHAT ARE THREE THINGS I'D IMPROVE?

1. _____
2. _____
3. _____

HOW DID I SUPPORT MY GOAL(S)?

_____
_____
_____
_____
_____
_____
_____
_____
_____
_____
_____
_____
_____
_____

WEEK:

GOAL OF THE WEEK:

MON
TUE
WED
THU
FRI
SAT
SUN

HOW DID THIS WEEK GO?

☆ ☆ ☆ ☆ ☆

CELEBRATE THREE WINS

1. _____

2. _____

3. _____

WHAT ARE THREE THINGS I'D IMPROVE?

1. _____

2. _____

3. _____

HOW DID I SUPPORT MY GOAL(S)?

_____

_____

_____

_____

_____

_____

_____

_____

_____

_____

_____

_____

_____

WEEK:

GOAL OF THE WEEK:

MON

TUE

WED

THU

FRI

SAT

SUN

HOW DID THIS WEEK GO?

☆ ☆ ☆ ☆ ☆

CELEBRATE THREE WINS

1. _____
2. _____
3. _____

WHAT ARE THREE THINGS I'D IMPROVE?

1. _____
2. _____
3. _____

HOW DID I SUPPORT MY GOAL(S)?

_____
_____
_____
_____
_____
_____
_____
_____
_____
_____
_____
_____

WEEK:

GOAL OF THE WEEK:

MON
TUE
WED
THU
FRI
SAT
SUN

HOW DID THIS WEEK GO?

☆ ☆ ☆ ☆ ☆

CELEBRATE THREE WINS

1. _____
2. _____
3. _____

WHAT ARE THREE THINGS I'D IMPROVE?

1. _____
2. _____
3. _____

HOW DID I SUPPORT MY GOAL(S)?

_____
_____
_____
_____
_____
_____
_____
_____
_____
_____
_____
_____
_____
_____

WEEK:

GOAL OF THE WEEK:

MON

TUE

WED

THU

FRI

SAT

SUN

HOW DID THIS WEEK GO?

☆ ☆ ☆ ☆ ☆

CELEBRATE THREE WINS

1. _____

2. _____

3. _____

WHAT ARE THREE THINGS I'D IMPROVE?

1. _____

2. _____

3. _____

HOW DID I SUPPORT MY GOAL(S)?

_____

_____

_____

_____

_____

_____

_____

_____

_____

_____

_____

_____

_____

MONTHLY REFLECTION

How closely did I stick to my habits this month?
(Circle one)

1	2	3	4	5
0%	25%	50%	75%	100%

Did I meet my monthly goal(s)? Why or why not?

_____

_____

_____

_____

_____

What went well this month?

_____

_____

_____

_____

_____

What do I want to work on next month?

_____

_____

_____

_____

_____

_____

Use this space to write out, draw, and reflect on your month.

MONTH:

GOAL OF THE MONTH:

SAT					
FRI					
THU					
WED					
TUE					
MON					
SUN					

MONTHLY CHALLENGE

Choose a few days this month to declutter these forgotten Clutter Catchers: your pantry, your medicine cabinet, your most used purse, your wallet, your desk at home or at work, your glove box, and your skincare or haircare. Set a timer for ten minutes each time and see how much you can get rid of!

SYMBOL KEY

Use these symbols to mark important occurrences and reminders on your calendar.

DAYS

$ Payday

$ No Buy day

D Declutter day

ONETIME EXPENSES

Travel

⚠ Emergency

M Maintenance

ESSENTIALS

🛒 Groceries

💊 Medication

🐾 Pet supplies

🏠 Home needs

RECURRING BILLS

$ Rent

💧 Utilities

📱 Phone

📶 Internet

$ Subscriptions

✚ Medical

Gym

% Loan

Credit Card

Car

% Mortgage

WEEK:

GOAL OF THE WEEK:

MON

TUE

WED

THU

FRI

SAT

SUN

HOW DID THIS WEEK GO?

☆ ☆ ☆ ☆ ☆

CELEBRATE THREE WINS

1. _____
2. _____
3. _____

WHAT ARE THREE THINGS I'D IMPROVE?

1. _____
2. _____
3. _____

HOW DID I SUPPORT MY GOAL(S)?

_____
_____
_____
_____
_____
_____
_____
_____
_____
_____
_____
_____
_____

WEEK:

GOAL OF THE WEEK:

MON

TUE

WED

THU

FRI

SAT

SUN

HOW DID THIS WEEK GO?

☆ ☆ ☆ ☆ ☆

CELEBRATE THREE WINS

1. _____
2. _____
3. _____

WHAT ARE THREE THINGS I'D IMPROVE?

1. _____
2. _____
3. _____

HOW DID I SUPPORT MY GOAL(S)?

_____
_____
_____
_____
_____
_____
_____
_____
_____
_____
_____
_____
_____
_____

WEEK:

GOAL OF THE WEEK:

MON
TUE
WED
THU
FRI
SAT
SUN

HOW DID THIS WEEK GO?

☆ ☆ ☆ ☆ ☆

CELEBRATE THREE WINS

1. _____
2. _____
3. _____

WHAT ARE THREE THINGS I'D IMPROVE?

1. _____
2. _____
3. _____

HOW DID I SUPPORT MY GOAL(S)?

_____
_____
_____
_____
_____
_____
_____
_____
_____
_____
_____
_____
_____

WEEK:

GOAL OF THE WEEK:

MON

TUE

WED

THU

FRI

SAT

SUN

HOW DID THIS WEEK GO?

☆ ☆ ☆ ☆ ☆

CELEBRATE THREE WINS

1. _____
2. _____
3. _____

WHAT ARE THREE THINGS I'D IMPROVE?

1. _____
2. _____
3. _____

HOW DID I SUPPORT MY GOAL(S)?

_____
_____
_____
_____
_____
_____
_____
_____
_____
_____
_____
_____
_____

WEEK:

GOAL OF THE WEEK:

MON
TUE
WED
THU
FRI
SAT
SUN

HOW DID THIS WEEK GO?

☆ ☆ ☆ ☆ ☆

CELEBRATE THREE WINS

1. _____
2. _____
3. _____

WHAT ARE THREE THINGS I'D IMPROVE?

1. _____
2. _____
3. _____

HOW DID I SUPPORT MY GOAL(S)?

_____
_____
_____
_____
_____
_____
_____
_____
_____
_____
_____
_____
_____

MONTHLY REFLECTION

How closely did I stick to my habits this month?
(Circle one)

1	2	3	4	5
0%	25%	50%	75%	100%

Did I meet my monthly goal(s)? Why or why not?

_____

_____

_____

_____

_____

What went well this month?

_____

_____

_____

_____

_____

What do I want to work on next month?

_____

_____

_____

_____

_____

_____

Use this space to write out, draw, and reflect on your month.

MONTH:

GOAL OF THE MONTH:

SAT					
FRI					
THU					
WED					
TUE					
MON					
SUN					

MONTHLY CHALLENGE

Challenge your limiting beliefs. What are some of the stories you tell yourself that may not necessarily be true? Write down three beliefs you have that may actually be holding you back. Now write the exact opposite of those beliefs. How does it feel to think about them differently? Can you change those beliefs?

SYMBOL KEY

Use these symbols to mark important occurrences and reminders on your calendar.

DAYS

$ Payday

✗ No Buy day

D Declutter day

ONETIME EXPENSES

💼 Travel

⚠ Emergency

M Maintenance

ESSENTIALS

🛒 Groceries

🐾 Pet supplies

🏠 Home needs

💊 Medication

RECURRING BILLS

🏠$ Rent

💧 Utilities

📱 Phone

📶 Internet

$✓ Subscriptions

✚ Medical

⊢⊣ Gym

% Loan

▭ Credit Card

🚗 Car

🏠% Mortgage

WEEK:

GOAL OF THE WEEK:

MON
TUE
WED
THU
FRI
SAT
SUN

HOW DID THIS WEEK GO?

☆ ☆ ☆ ☆ ☆

CELEBRATE THREE WINS

1. _____
2. _____
3. _____

WHAT ARE THREE THINGS I'D IMPROVE?

1. _____
2. _____
3. _____

HOW DID I SUPPORT MY GOAL(S)?

_____
_____
_____
_____
_____
_____
_____
_____
_____
_____
_____
_____
_____
_____

WEEK:

GOAL OF THE WEEK:

MON
TUE
WED
THU
FRI
SAT
SUN

HOW DID THIS WEEK GO?

☆ ☆ ☆ ☆ ☆

CELEBRATE THREE WINS

1. _____
2. _____
3. _____

WHAT ARE THREE THINGS I'D IMPROVE?

1. _____
2. _____
3. _____

HOW DID I SUPPORT MY GOAL(S)?

_____
_____
_____
_____
_____
_____
_____
_____
_____
_____
_____
_____
_____
_____

WEEK:

GOAL OF THE WEEK:

MON
TUE
WED
THU
FRI
SAT
SUN

HOW DID THIS WEEK GO?

☆ ☆ ☆ ☆ ☆

CELEBRATE THREE WINS

1. _____
2. _____
3. _____

WHAT ARE THREE THINGS I'D IMPROVE?

1. _____
2. _____
3. _____

HOW DID I SUPPORT MY GOAL(S)?

_____
_____
_____
_____
_____
_____
_____
_____
_____
_____
_____
_____
_____
_____

WEEK:

GOAL OF THE WEEK:

MON

TUE

WED

THU

FRI

SAT

SUN

HOW DID THIS WEEK GO?

☆ ☆ ☆ ☆ ☆

CELEBRATE THREE WINS

1. _____
2. _____
3. _____

WHAT ARE THREE THINGS I'D IMPROVE?

1. _____
2. _____
3. _____

HOW DID I SUPPORT MY GOAL(S)?

_____
_____
_____
_____
_____
_____
_____
_____
_____
_____
_____
_____
_____
_____

WEEK:

GOAL OF THE WEEK:

MON
TUE
WED
THU
FRI
SAT
SUN

HOW DID THIS WEEK GO?

☆ ☆ ☆ ☆ ☆

CELEBRATE THREE WINS

1. _____
2. _____
3. _____

WHAT ARE THREE THINGS I'D IMPROVE?

1. _____
2. _____
3. _____

HOW DID I SUPPORT MY GOAL(S)?

_____
_____
_____
_____
_____
_____
_____
_____
_____
_____
_____
_____
_____
_____
_____

MONTHLY REFLECTION

How closely did I stick to my habits this month?
(Circle one)

1	2	3	4	5
0%	25%	50%	75%	100%

Did I meet my monthly goal(s)? Why or why not?

_____

_____

_____

_____

_____

What went well this month?

_____

_____

_____

_____

What do I want to work on next month?

_____

_____

_____

_____

_____

_____

Use this space to write out, draw, and reflect on your month.

QUARTERLY REFLECTION

My wins over the last three months

_____

_____

_____

Habits that are supporting my goals

_____

_____

_____

_____

Three things I realized I'm grateful for

1. _____

2. _____

3. _____

Three things I was happy to let go of

1. _____

2. _____

3. _____

One thing I want to do next. Why? How?

_____

_____

_____

_____

_____

_____

_____

_____

_____

Use this space to write out, draw, and reflect on the last three months.

END-OF-YEAR REFLECTION

Congratulations! You made it! Use this spread to reflect back on your year. Remember, Minimalist-ish and intentional living are ongoing practices. You live, you learn, and you adjust as you go. Progress over perfection, always!

My top three accomplishments

1. _____
2. _____
3. _____

Three things I would change about last year

1. _____
2. _____
3. _____

Three things I want to achieve next year

1. _____
2. _____
3. _____

New habits I plan to carry into next year

_____
_____
_____
_____
_____
_____

Three things I still need to work on

1. _____
2. _____
3. _____

One thing or experience I want to splurge on next year

_____
_____
_____
_____
_____
_____
_____
_____
_____
_____
_____

WISH LIST

BEFORE BUYING, I WILL WAIT (Circle one):

1 DAY | 1 WEEK | 1 MONTH | 1 YEAR

WANT	HOW MUCH	WHY I WANT IT
~~Luxury bag~~	~~$500~~	~~It will elevate any look I wear~~

BEFORE BUYING, I WILL WAIT (Circle one):

1 DAY | 1 WEEK | 1 MONTH | 1 YEAR

WANT	HOW MUCH	WHY I WANT IT

WISH LIST ITEM PLANNER

GOAL ITEM	COST	SAVINGS PER MONTH
Luxury bag	$500	$50

STARTING BALANCE	DURATION	TARGET DATE
$0	10 months	01/01/2026

INVENTORY TRACKER

CATEGORY:

ITEM	QUANTITY	NOTES

CATEGORY:

ITEM	QUANTITY	NOTES

CATEGORY:

ITEM	QUANTITY	NOTES

CATEGORY:

ITEM	QUANTITY	NOTES

CATEGORY:

ITEM	QUANTITY	NOTES

CATEGORY:

ITEM	QUANTITY	NOTES

about the author

Christina Mychas is a content creator, entrepreneur, and writer. A self-described shopaholic, she created the Minimalist-ish® Method to change her emotional spending habits and face the financial mess she always felt stuck in. Through her social media channels, she helps others do the same. She lives in Toronto, Canada.